You Write It

Creative Writing for GCSE English and Other Examinations

Gordon Michael Sutton

© Gordon Michael Sutton 2019

All rights reserved. No part of this publication may be reproduced, stored in a retrieval system, or transmitted in any form or by any means, electronic, mechanical, photocopying, recording or otherwise, without the prior permission in writing of the publisher, except in the case of brief quotations embodied in a book review.

ISBN: 978-1-9160147-0-1 (Paperback)
ISBN: 978-1-9160147-1-8 (Kindle)

Image page 4 – Supplied and copyright to PA Images

Typesetting – Chris Moore www.fromprinttoebook.com

Dedication

To my wife, Liz, for her boundless encouragement
and optimism, and my grown up children,
Alex and Will, for believing in their Dad.

Contents

Dedication..iii

Acknowledgements..vii

How to use this book...viii

Introduction..1

Section 1 Narrative Writing 3

Look, imagine and plan..4

Start with a bang..8

Choosing a narrative voice..................................10

Introduce a little direct speech............................12

Let's focus on the content of the paragraph........12

How to use dialogue in your narrative writing......16

Practise writing dialogue....................................21

Creating characters in narrative writing...............24

Remember – characters have feelings!................27

Thinking about your characters in more detail....31

Contrasting characters in narrative writing..........34

Abingdon Square Park 40

Structure 44

Narrative Writing – Exemplar 1 54

Narrative Writing – Exemplar 2 56

Narrative Writing – Exemplar 3 59

SECTION 2   DESCRIPTIVE WRITING 65

First steps with descriptive writing 66

Some ideas for using the senses in descriptive writing 69

Now it's your turn 74

Descriptive writing – first responses to a photograph 76

Descriptive writing – shifting the perspective 79

Interrogating the image 85

Collating your responses to photographs 89

Descriptive Writing – Exemplar 1 92

Descriptive Writing – Exemplar 2 95

Descriptive Writing – Exemplar 3 98

Acknowledgements

I'd like to thank the following for their invaluable help and expertise:

The community of fellow professionals at Avenue HQ in Liverpool for their advice, support and good humour (https://www.avenue-hq.com).

Hannah, Lily and Olivia – friends and family – who gave me honest and constructive feedback on the penultimate draft of the book.

Finally, the many students I've had the privilege to teach, not forgetting my fellow English specialists in schools, academies and local authorities in the UK and overseas who I've been fortunate to engage with over the years.

Gordon
January, 2019

How to use this book

I've written and designed this book to be as authentic as possible, filling it with plenty of my own examples of tackling the writing process itself as well as completed responses to typical exam questions. There are also detailed, commentaries on each of the six exemplars of creative writing to help you understand some of their key strengths and features.

My goal has been to develop your confidence, enthusiasm and motivation as writers so I've worked hard to make sure the content of the book is as colourful and attractive as possible, including the careful selection of interesting and appropriate photographs. Photographs, in my view, are really important in providing a visual stimulus for helping to develop creative writing. They're also important, of course, because you're often going to find that you have to produce creative writing in an examination in response to a photograph.

The book has been divided into two sections – ***Narrative Writing*** and ***Descriptive Writing***. Each section follows a similar step-by-step approach, with careful explanations of the various strategies that can be used to develop your skills along the way.

Most important of all, the book offers you regular opportunities to have a go at creative writing – hence the title – ***You** Write It*.

Key

- Summary of key points and ideas

- Instructions

- Exam questions or titles

- Examples of my writing + Exemplar responses to exam questions

- Commentary on Exemplar responses to exam questions

- Space for your written responses and ideas

Introduction

Thank you for purchasing '*You Write It – Creative Writing for GCSE English and other examinations.*'

This is a book about the process of creative writing which includes examples of my own work, both narrative and descriptive in which I've tried to tackle the sort of questions you're likely to encounter in your English exam.

I enjoyed writing this book and being able to share with you some of the ways you can impr ove the quality of your own creative writing.

I hope it might also inspire you to enjoy the writing process and to develop your own authentic ideas and approaches.

I've tried to apply a number of principles when writing this book:

- To make it as readable and accessible as possible
- To make it visually interesting
- To offer practical advice and guidance that you can follow easily and apply in your own writing
- To provide plenty of examples of both descriptive and narrative writing with a commentary
- To share my thinking process and the choices I've made as a writer

Follow me on
Instagram : **secretsofenglish**
Twitter : **@secretsofengli1**
http://www.secretsofenglish.co.uk

"I've always associated the moment of writing with a moment of lift, of joy, of unexpected reward. I always believed that whatever had to be written would somehow get itself written."

Seamus Heaney

Section 1

Narrative Writing

Look, imagine and plan

Examiners like using photos as the stimulus for a piece of narrative and/or descriptive writing. This sounds great in theory but sometimes the photos aren't necessarily the most interesting or exciting. So it's your job to make the best of what you're given. You can do this by following 3 steps.

1. **Look carefully at the image**
2. **Activate your imagination**
3. **Plan**

Let me show you what I mean with a little help from the photo below. As is often the case, you may have a choice of narrative or descriptive writing as follows:

(A) Write the opening part of a story about how wintry conditions play a part in people's lives

or

(B) Write a piece of description suggested by the photograph.

I've decided to tackle this as a piece of ***narrative*** writing.

Step 1: Look carefully at the image you're given.

Don't hang around or try to think too hard. Just get stuck in.

Here's my quick list:

- Winter
- Heavy snow
- Overhanging branches of trees
- Lights of cars
- Traffic queueing + exhaust fumes
- Footprints in the snow
- Main character … paperboy … high-vis bag

Step 2: Activate your imagination.

At this stage, I'm still jotting ideas down before starting to write. Notice that I've written some of my ideas as questions. This is to help me to do some thinking about what I want to use in my story.

- 1st person narrator/paperboy
- Paper round/discovery in the snow?
- Paperboy family background – not very well off, maybe?
- Chance find in the snow? A wallet stuffed with cash and credit cards plus ID?
- Family of paper boy … mother + younger brother + old grandmother – ill and infirm.
- Paper round in quite a rough area.
- How did the wallet get there? Stolen? Accident?

Equipped with the two lists above it's time to think about shaping my ideas.

Step 3: Plan

There are many ways you can plan but I've decided to draft a numerical paragraph plan: This is what I've settled on. Remember to keep a paragraph plan nice and simple.

> **P1** – Background info on the boy
> **P2** – Typical early morning paper round (rush hour)
> **P3** – Snow ball exchange … (dialogue) … 'the discovery'
> **P4** – At home with breakfast … pondering his find/wallet
> **P5** – Reminder of poverty/family/grandma … seeks her advice/shares the discovery … first thoughts are to spend the cash … but!!!
> **P6** – ?

Notice that I'm not too sure where the narrative is going in Paragraph 6 at this stage. Some of you might want to have that pinned down before you start writing. For me, it's going to allow for some spontaneous choices as the story progresses about where it's going next. This is very much a matter of personal preference though. So this is the start of what I've written. See what you think.

> *Josh was only fifteen. Sometimes he felt like he was fifty.*
>
> *Peering out of the frozen window at the snow below, today of all days, he certainly didn't feel too enthusiastic about setting out on his early morning paper round. He'd had a heavy cold for a week or two now and the council flat he shared with his mum and grandma made matters worse; heating the tiny flat hadn't been an option for his mum as she struggled to get by on the benefits she received. The weekly contribution to the family kitty from Josh's paper round was vital.*
>
> *Five minutes into his mundane, daily route and Josh's cheeks were numb from the biting cold wind; even his bedroom in the chilly flat would be preferable to these wintry conditions! Weighed down by the heavy bag on his shoulders, Josh knew today's walk wasn't going to be easy. The fumes from the queuing cars had started to sting his eyes; most days he wouldn't notice that. Neither would he normally find his eyes distracted by the bright red glow of the cars' taillights as they slowly shunted and edged forward down the road.*

Josh trudged onwards. With every lumbering footstep, he could hear his boots crunching in the deep snow.

"Oy, mate, take that!"

Before he knew what was happening, a cold, wet snowball had hit Josh square on his nose. Without giving it a second thought, Josh bent down and moulded a solid ball of snow, eager to retaliate. He could easily anticipate the reaction from the other boy, as he watched his snowball head towards him. This snow ball fight was turning into a free for all! Josh readied himself for the next onslaught and started to gather some more snow in his hands. But something wasn't quite right.

Try as hard as he might, Josh struggled in frustration as he attempted to make another snowball. If he wasn't quick, he'd end up getting clobbered by another one himself.

Glancing down at his frozen hands, he was puzzled to see a dark, stained and soggy object and was ready to hurl it away. But something told him not to. Brushing the snow away, he quickly realised that what he'd found was a wallet stuffed with bank cards and cash. Without hesitation, Josh, as if following his instinct, stashed the wallet in the back pocket of his jeans.

"Alright, mate, you win," Josh hollered at his adversary.

He was keen to return home to take a proper look at the treasure he'd found.

Why not try to write the next paragraph?

Start with a bang

I can't stress enough how important an interesting and thought-provoking open line can be in a piece of *narrative writing*. It's all about catching your reader's attention.

Think of it as the bait on the hook; once they've bitten, you can start to reel your readers in.

What you should try to avoid at all costs is leaving your readers floundering around and wondering what the story's about. Readers can get bored very quickly and that can be deadly for you as the writer. Your examiner is your reader, too, don't forget!

The image above is the starting point for my next narrative piece by the way.

> **Remember to use the *3 steps* we looked at in the previous section**

In this short narrative attempt, I wanted to inject a little mystery into a mundane situation; a beach, some sunshine, and a chance to relax. Nothing to see there you might think.

Here's my opening line:

> *The last drops of suntan lotion were dripping from the bottle onto the open paperback.*

Something's not quite right by the sound of it, is it?

I'm hoping I've got my reader wondering why a bottle of suntan lotion has been left to drip onto an open paperback book that they might presume somebody has been reading recently.

And as for them being the "***last drops***", has the bottle been dripping like this for some time? Or maybe it's because somebody's nearly reached the end of their holiday?

Of course, it could be the result of a simple accident, but at this stage the readers aren't sure. To answer the questions I've raised they'll need to read on.

It's all about arousing curiosity you see.

Here's that opening line again:

> *The last drops of suntan lotion were dripping from the bottle onto the open paperback.*

http://www.secretsofenglish.co.uk

Choosing a narrative voice

As you put pen to paper with your narrative writing you should be weighing up how you're going to tell the story.

Q: From whose perspective will it be written?

Q: Is it going to be a first or third person narrative?

Here's the opening paragraph from my writing, including the opening line that we've just been looking at:

> *The last drops of suntan lotion were dripping from the bottle onto the open paperback. Michael was nowhere to be seen. He'd warned me often enough about the need to be on his guard to make me realise that something wasn't quite right here. I was beginning to suspect he might have vanished.*

I've wasted no time introducing my central character and I've reinforced the sense of mystery as well.

> *Michael was nowhere to be seen.*

But it's clear that I'm writing this as a first person narrative – and I'm writing about Michael.

I've not yet revealed who the "*I*" in the story is though. Who's the person telling the story and how is he or she connected to Michael?

As early as the third sentence I've started to make it clear to the reader that there is some sort of relationship. That they know each other. In fact, my narrator reveals an important detail that adds to the suspense and concern that I'm building in the mind of the readers.

> *He'd warned me often enough about the need to be on his guard to make me realise that something wasn't quite right here.*

My narrator is already beginning to think and behave like a detective as he tries to track Michael down.

And tracking Michael down is the objective of my narrative in fact.

If I can handle this properly, my readers will stay with me. Why? Because they want to find Michael too. Just a few sentences into my narrative and they've started to invest their thoughts and feelings into Michael's wellbeing.

I think I'm well on my way to achieving this goal, especially with the final line of the first paragraph:

*I was beginning to suspect he might have **vanished**.*

I want everything to hang on that word 'vanished'.

It could mean almost anything as far as Michael's fate is concerned. One thing's for sure – something's wrong and you'll need to read on to find out more.

Introduce a little direct speech

My next paragraph has a different job to do and it doesn't hang around. It starts to shift the narrative forward quite quickly. The pace is quickening.

> *Of course, he'd vanished once or twice before, but usually turned up having been for a lengthy swim or for a drink in a bar further down the beach. A quick check back at my own beach bar confirmed that our paths hadn't crossed and that he hadn't been back there.*
>
> *"Pedro, take care of the customers, I'll be back soon," I said to the bartender and set off to look for Mike further down the beach.*

I've included another photo just to help make the explanation of my writing process a little clearer. It also helps to emphasise the value of thinking visually when you produce any narrative writing too. The photo is a reminder that my mysterious missing person narrative is actually rooted in quite ordinary circumstances – a relaxed and easygoing beach bar in this instance.

Let's focus on the content of the paragraph.

- I'm giving my readers a glimpse into the mind of my narrator as he tries to re-assure himself that Michael has "*vanished once or twice before*".

- You may remember a little while back that my narrator was starting to think and behave like a detective. I've let him drop a few details into the narrative that encourage the reader to see him in this light again.

- His use of the word "***usually***", for example, drops a subtle hint that Michael is quite well known here and must have been a regular visitor of some sort. This is a good example of how a first person narrator can help to influence and shape the reader's perceptions and understanding of the plot.

- The narrator also mentions that Michael had been known to go for a "*lengthy swim*" – it makes him sound like he was quite a fit individual. So it's unlikely he's got into trouble while swimming.

- My narrator is torn between a growing concern for Michael's wellbeing and the possibility that there's a simple, obvious reason for him vanishing.
- I've included a few details about swimming and the beach bar to help make the scene I've created more credible in the minds of the reader. They also add to the sense of this being just a normal day at an ordinary beach bar.
- The main feature that I'd like you to notice, though, is my use of a line of direct speech at the end of the paragraph:

"Pedro, take care of the customers, I'll be back soon," I said to the bartender and set off to look for Mike further down the beach.

- I've been trying hard so far to convince readers that my narrative's a credible one. I want them to inhabit the world and to become concerned about Michael's fate. By using just a little direct speech, I've suddenly brought this tale to life by allowing my narrator's voice to be heard. I've made it just that little bit more realistic, more convincing – and that can make all the difference to the success of your narrative writing.

I mentioned at the start of this section that I wanted to shift the narrative forward quite quickly. Having ended his short piece of direct speech, I've had my narrator tell the reader that he's now heading off "*further down the beach*" on his search for Michael.

One more thing.

- Did you notice that my narrator is now referring to him as "*Mike*" instead of "*Michael*" – just a little clue I've slipped into the narrative that they must have known each other pretty well, which also helps to explain the narrator's concern.

Fortunately the beach had emptied in the scorching mid-day heat which made searching that much easier. I must have walked a good mile or so and hadn't spotted a soul on the bright, shimmering sand. Without realising it, I found that I found myself wandering along in the warm, white surf as it hit the shore. Perhaps it was the noise of the waves that first caused my gaze to turn out to sea.

Now you write the next couple of paragraphs.

How to use dialogue in your narrative writing

Look back over your day and think about all the times you've heard people talking to each other. Maybe it was a couple of teachers chatting in the school corridor. Or perhaps it was friends having a catch up on the bus. It might even have been your family over the breakfast table at home this morning.

Sometimes people want to ask questions. Sometimes they need to tell you something. Sometimes they want to discuss things.

It's a common feature of everyday life.

For this reason alone, it's a good idea to use some dialogue – or talk between characters – in any narrative writing you produce.

But remember, any dialogue you use should have a purpose which could be one or more of the following:

- It can be used to help reveal information about a character by the things they say, and how they say them
- It can be used to boost or slow down the pace of your story, depending on what's being said
- It can be used to increase tension and drama in your story

Take a look at **Extract A** and **Extract B** below to see what I mean.

Extract A

> *The light had started to fade as the two friends strolled across the bridge. It had been at least a year since they'd seen each other and they had much to catch up on. The noise of the traffic made conversation difficult as they made their way onto the busy high street. Nevertheless, they talked all the way. It was always good to catch up like this. A problem shared was a problem halved.*

Extract B.

The light had started to fade as the two friends strolled across the bridge. It had been at least a year since they'd seen each other and they had much to catch up on.

"It's not been easy," Ella whispered.

"I expect so," replied Lucy, "how did you cope?"

The noise of the traffic made conversation difficult as they made their way onto the busy high street.

"I had no choice … Mum just went to pieces after Dad died and someone had to be strong."

"That must have been so hard. I can't imagine how you held it all together."

"You just do. You just have to," Ella said.

Before they knew it, they found that they'd been talking all the way down the long street.

It was always good to catch up like this, Lucy thought. A problem shared was a problem halved.

Question: What extra information have you learned from Extract B that you didn't get in Extract A?

Question: In your opinion, has the dialogue in Extract B slowed down or increased the pace in your narrative?

Question: In what way has tension or drama been increased through the use of dialogue in Extract B?

Hopefully you will have noticed from **Extract A** and **Extract B** that I've not allowed the dialogue to run away with itself. In fact, I've used just enough dialogue to make a difference. It's a bit like riding a horse, I suppose. You need to show the horse who's the boss and keep a firm hand on the reins. When you produce your piece of narrative writing in the exam, you need to show the examiner that you're in control of the writing and you're using dialogue selectively.

Let's take a closer look at how we can use dialogue to good effect in our narrative writing. Here are a few more things you should try to do:

- Keep any dialogue short, concise and to the point
- Don't over-use the word '*said*' in your dialogue … try to find alternatives
- Try to create a unique 'voice' for each of your characters who speak during the story – think carefully about how they'd speak and the sort of language they'd use

One more point that I think is too important to ignore right now:

- You may want your narrative writing to include confrontation between your characters at some point.

I'm going to try to do all of that in **Extract C** below. Before you take a look at it though, here's a little background about what I want to write.

The dialogue I'm going to write will be inserted into a narrative about an unlikely pair of school friends. Freddie, the larger of the two, is quite brash, popular and outgoing, whilst Theo is the studious type and much more reserved. We'll join the narrative as the two friends, Freddie and Theo, stop off in a local coffee shop on the way home from school. It's been a busy week and they're both piled up with revision as the exams are getting closer. It's now getting late on a Friday afternoon and they're discussing their plans for the weekend ahead. Here goes.

Extract C.

Theo made his way through the busy crowd of seated customers careful not to barge into anyone with his backpack, or spill any of the coffee he was clutching in his hand. It always amused him how their favourite seats, tucked away near the noisy, hissing espresso machine always seemed to be free and today was no exception.

"Here, grab this!" Freddie shouted.

Theo looked up from his phone to see Freddie looming above, shoving his coffee cup at him.

"Just grab it will you. Quick!" Freddie yelled.

Theo reached forward, took the cardboard coffee cup and placed it on the table in front of him. Before he had a chance to protest, Freddie had vanished in the direction of the toilets.

"What's the face for?" Freddie said, when he returned, goading Theo.

The two had been friends since primary school and knew each other well but recently Theo had started to find Freddie's behaviour irritating to say the least.

"Never mind my face, what's that haircut for?" Theo retorted.

Freddie had recently taken to wearing his hair in a top-knot bun and thought he looked pretty cool. Theo just thought he looked ridiculous.

"Shut it, Muppet!"

"I'm not the one with an onion on my head, you're the Muppet," replied Theo.

"I'd watch what you're saying if I were you," Freddie warned.

As you can see from **Extract C** above, things have started to escalate quite quickly between the two friends. I hope you'll agree that I've also managed to create two very different voices that reflect the characters themselves, one abrupt and rude towards his friend, the other quite passive at first but who gradually speaks up for himself.

It's Freddie's harsh words, almost spat out, that do most to create a sense of confrontation between the friends. Notice that I've used exclamation marks to add a little emphasis to his words.

His final words to Theo are uttered with a nasty, threatening edge to them and my readers ought to be keen to read on to see what happens next. So now, let's remind ourselves of the checklist for using dialogue effectively in narrative writing and see how **Extract C** measures up:

- It can be used to help reveal information about a character by the things they say, and how they say them
- It can be used to boost or slow down the pace of your story, depending on what's being said
- It can be used to increase tension and drama in your story
- Keep any dialogue short, concise and to the point
- Don't over-use the word 'said' in your dialogue
- Try to create a unique 'voice' for each of your characters who speak during the story – think carefully about how they'd speak and the sort of language they'd use
- You may want your narrative writing to include some confrontation between your characters at some point.

What do you think? How many of the above have I managed to do in **Extract C**?

Practise writing dialogue

1.

- Study the photo above and imagine that one of the characters has a secret – something they don't want the other person to know.
- Now imagine that the other character has something that they want to reveal but are struggling to say. It's probably a good idea if you can work out what's on their minds before you put pen to paper.
- Both have their reasons for not wanting to talk but eventually they start communicating with each other.
- Once you have a clear picture of who they are in your mind and you have a good idea of what their voices sound like, try to write a piece of dialogue between them.

2.

Choose one of the following and try to write about one side of A4. You don't have to know who the characters are, where they are, or why they're at odds:

- "I think I've caught your cold."
- "Why don't you just admit that you're wrong?"
- "There's no point getting upset about things."
- "It's probably best if you told them the truth."
- "What's the matter with you?"

3.

Read the following piece of writing. Now try to rewrite it, correcting the dialogue. Remember to start each person's words on a new line.

It'll work said Jackson it'll definitely work how can you be so sure asked Hamda trust me, I know what I'm talking about said Jackson that's all well and good but unless you can show me the proof then I can't go along with this harebrained idea Hamda replied anxiously well that's up to you said Jackson look I'm sorry to let you down said Hamda but that's all there is to it.

Remember to start each new speaker on a new line.

4.

In this exercise, try to recall a recent conversation or chat you've had with somebody you know well – maybe a friend, a teacher, or a member of your family. First, just jot down the actual words that were used in the conversation as far as you can remember them. Next, re-read it and try to include some details of how the speakers spoke to each other as they were talking, including any mannerisms they might have.

If you're stuck, maybe write the conversation that the people in the photograph below might have.

Now have a go at one of the exercises above in the space below.

Creating characters in narrative writing

You'd think creating a couple of characters in a piece of narrative writing would be easy enough. After all, there are people around us all the time; on the bus, on the high street, not to mention in school.

A few years ago I was lucky enough to travel to Beijing in China and on the first morning in the hotel, I was fascinated by this image of two Chinese men deep in conversation over their breakfast. The image caught my eye because they're almost just silhouettes – we can't see much more about them. How could I bring them to life and turn them into convincing characters?

Sometimes the narrative question in the GCSE English exam – the one where you're asked to write a story – will specifically ask you to write about a couple of *contrasting characters.*

The exam board will be doing this deliberately.

They want to see that not only can you create **one** interesting and convincing character, but that you can use your imagination to create **a second one** who's quite different.

And because it's a story – a piece of narrative writing – you might want to think about including some sort of **conflict or opposition** between your characters. This will help to engage your reader – help to get them involved in the lives of your characters and the situation they find themselves in.

Conflict helps to make a story more dramatic, too – it will make your reader sit up and pay attention!

So where are you going to get your ideas from when it comes to creating and writing about your characters? How are you going to start this story?

To return to the photo above, I'm really going to need to flesh out the two characters to make them convincing.

Take a look at these 3 steps for creating interesting characters:

Step 1. Plan your story first

- You're writing a story that needs to fill about 2 to 3 sides of A4 paper – it helps if you can show you're in control of the story from start to finish
- A plan will help you to have an overview of the whole story before you start to write it and prevent you from either running out of ideas, or rambling and running out of time
- A good plan will enable you to design when, where and how your characters meet and interact
- The plan will also allow you to think through the events of your story and how these involve your characters – particularly as events might build towards some sort of conflict and resolution – it will help to make your characters shine and make your characters strong and convincing.

- The exam as a whole will have given you the chance to analyse how a writer structures his/her work and planning will allow you to think how to structure your own writing so as to make maximum impact on your reader.

Step 2. Give each of your characters a unique identity

- Who are they? What is their gender?
- What motivates them – greed, jealousy, or hatred maybe? Or perhaps it's generosity, kindness, or compassion? Or something else altogether?
- Develop their identities. Are they old or young? What do they look like? What are their occupations? There are endless choices to be made. Don't spend too much time worrying about this. Keep things fairly simple.

Step 3. Make them memorable

- It's down to you to give your characters names – if you make their names too ordinary, your characters could become instantly forgettable – on the other hand, if you make the names too strange or unusual, your readers may struggle to relate to them.
- Give your character a trait or characteristic that makes them stand out – maybe one of your characters has the habit of sniffing when they're nervous … or maybe one of them likes to have a few too many teaspoons of sugar in their coffee – strange habits such as these can help to endear a character to your reader.
- The last thing you want is for your characters to seem one-dimensional or flat – so think through how to develop an interesting personality for them that the reader will be able to recognise in everything your characters do and say.

Remember – characters have feelings!

Credible and interesting characters are at the heart of a good piece of narrative writing so it's important to try to show some human feelings and emotions in the ones you've created to inhabit your stories. This will also help to make for a more powerful narrative as these feelings and emotions can often provide the motivation for a character's actions and responses. But first, you'll need to decide what sort of feelings and emotions they might be.

Here are a few images of individuals each experiencing some sort of emotion.

Take a look at this first picture and see what emotion you think he's experiencing.

Can you think of any other words to describe that emotion?

What were the clues in the photograph that helped you to identify the emotion?

Now take a look at this second image.

What's the feeling or emotion being shown here?

Is the feeling being shown here more, or less intense, than the one shown in the first photograph? Why do you think this is?

Now use your imagination and try to provide a reason why the man in this second photograph is feeling like this? Has something happened to make him feel this way?

Now imagine he's the main character in your story. How will your second character respond to him? Imagine what a short piece of dialogue between them might look and sound like.

Now here's a third photograph for you to think about.

Choose one of the 3 photographs above and write the first few paragraphs of a story in which your main character's feelings and emotions play a part.

Thinking about your characters in more detail

We've already taken a look at characters and their feelings on pages 27 - 29.

As part of your planning for a narrative piece of writing, it's worth jotting down a brief character sketch or profile for your two main characters.

Using the images below to help you, build your profiles using the following bullet points:

- Jot down the feeling or emotion that the person in the image seems to be showing. Remember, it might be a mixture of emotions, so write down what you think
- Now look back at the emotion (or emotions) you've jotted down above, and try to write down a few alternative words for these
- Look closely at each photo again. What were the clues in each image that helped you to identify the emotion (or emotions)
- Now use your imagination and write down the reasons why the person in each image is feeling the way they are
- Now invent a character trait for each character
- Finally, try to create a name for each character

Image 1

Thinking about your characters in more detail

Image 2

Contrasting characters in narrative writing

I thought now might be a good time for me to share a piece of my own writing in which I'm trying to put my ideas into practice.

My aim is to create two contrasting characters who are brought together in slightly unusual circumstances. First, I want to create a narrative in which details of the main character and her situation are *gradually* revealed.

Here goes.

> "The Infirmary, please."
>
> Mrs Jackson pulled as hard as she could to shut the taxi door. Settling herself onto the broad, back seat of the taxi, Edna let out a gentle sigh and closed her eyes. It had been another long and wearying day.
>
> It had all revolved around cups of tea and eating the occasional slice of toast. After a light lunch of chicken soup and a Kit Kat biscuit, Edna had set off for the first of her two daily visits to the Infirmary to see Bert, her husband of nearly sixty years. Not only was she missing him badly but this new routine was taking some adjusting to. It was beginning to take its toll on her.
>
> She hadn't been sleeping too well in an empty house and had found herself more tired than usual during the day. Bert had also done the lion's share of the cooking for quite a few years now and if Edna was entirely honest with herself, she hadn't been eating properly since he'd become poorly a couple of weeks ago.

I've got my narrative moving quickly – it's about a taxi ride taken by an old woman to see her sick husband in the local hospital. Without slowing my narrative down, I've also introduced the first of my two characters – Edna.

If my readers have been paying attention, I've given them plenty of information about her already, to help them relate to her character and her circumstances.

Here's what you may have picked up about her:

- polite – "please"
- married – "Mrs Jackson"
- frail – "pulled as hard as she could"
- tired – "let out a gentle sigh and closed her eyes"
- her diet – cups of tea, chicken soup, Kit Kats, toast – not eating properly
- married for nearly 60 years
- missing her husband and struggling to adjust
- dependent on her husband – "the lion's share of the cooking"

I've managed to do all that in just 14 lines of writing.

The next challenge is to keep the narrative moving and introduce my second character, who I want to be very different from Edna. Here goes:

"Is everything alright, Ma'am?"

Edna was suddenly aware of a man's voice coming from the front of the cab. She noticed that they'd stopped at the lights of a busy junction.

"Erm. Fine thank you," she replied.

"You seem a little tired?" said the man.

Edna took a moment or two before replying and tried to weigh up the taxi driver.

He was wearing a yellow turban.

A greying beard.

Blue checked shirt.

She had to admit to herself that his voice sounded kind and oddly reassuring. She couldn't for the life of her remember who it was who wore turbans.

> *Amarjot's brown eyes glanced in his rear view mirror, a little anxious about his elderly passenger. Perhaps wait to see if she replied first, he thought. He'd been a taxi driver for eight years now and had seen it all from the front of his cab.*
>
> *He prided himself on being a well presented and well-mannered driver who could put his passengers at their ease and, as a Sikh, respect for his elders had also been instilled in him from his boyhood.*
>
> *"Mrs Jackson? Are you alright?" he asked again, as the cab moved off into the traffic towards the hospital.*

Have I done what I set out to do?

Yes, I've kept the narrative moving.

My main character is a little closer to her destination – the Infirmary – to visit her sick husband.

I've also created a relationship of sorts between Edna and Amarjot, the Sikh taxi driver, by using a little dialogue between them. This, in turn, helps to create some tension and drama by posing a few questions; why is Edna reluctant to engage with Amarjot? why does she feel the need to scrutinise him as she does? why is Amarjot so concerned?

I also wanted my second character to be quite different to Edna.

Well, I've given him a Sikh identity for starters, which immediately sets Amarjot and Edna a little apart. Her curiosity about him – about his turban and beard – also hint at this 'otherness'.

I've also tried to create a picture of Amarjot as a kind, compassionate individual through his concern for Edna's well-being.

Finally, I've made an explicit reference to his Sikh faith and culture by stressing the importance that is placed on showing respect for your elders.

And that's it for now.

I've left plenty of scope to develop this relationship between Edna and Amarjot as they continue on their journey to the Infirmary.

Q. What part might Amarjot come to play as they reach their destination?

Q. How much will Edna reveal about her new circumstances to Amarjot?

Q. How can I continue to show the differences between them?

Q. How can I demonstrate a common bond between them?

Here are the two extracts joined together.

> *"The Infirmary, please."*
>
> *Mrs Jackson pulled as hard as she could to shut the taxi door. Settling herself onto the broad back seat of the taxi, Edna let out a gentle sigh and closed her eyes. It had been another long and wearying day.*
>
> *It had all revolved around cups of tea and eating the occasional slice of toast. After a light lunch of chicken soup and a Kit Kat biscuit, Edna had set off for the first of her two daily visits to the Infirmary to see Bert, her husband of nearly sixty years. Not only was she missing him badly but this new routine was taking some adjusting to. It was beginning to take its toll on her.*
>
> *She hadn't been sleeping too well in an empty house and had found herself more tired than usual during the day. Bert had also done the lion's share of the cooking for quite a few years now and if Edna was entirely honest with herself, she hadn't been eating properly since he'd become poorly a couple of weeks ago.*
>
> *"Is everything alright, Ma'am?"*
>
> *Edna was suddenly aware of a man's voice coming from the front of the cab. She noticed that they'd stopped at the lights at a busy junction.*
>
> *"Erm. Fine thank you," she replied.*
>
> *"You seem a little tired?" said the man.*
>
> *Edna took a moment or two before replying and tried to weigh up the taxi driver.*
>
> *He was wearing a yellow turban.*
>
> *A greying beard.*

Blue checked shirt.

She had to admit to herself that his voice sounded kind and oddly reassuring. She couldn't for the life of her remember who it was who wore turbans.

Amarjot's brown eyes glanced in his rear view mirror, a little anxious about his elderly passenger. Perhaps wait to see if she replied first, he thought. He'd been a taxi driver for eight years now and had seen it all from the front of his cab.

He prided himself on being a well presented and well-mannered driver who could put his passengers at their ease and as a Sikh, respect for his elders had also been instilled in him from his boyhood.

"Mrs Jackson? Are you alright?" he asked again, as the cab moved off into the traffic towards the hospital.

Why don't you try to continue the story of Edna and Amarjot?

Abingdon Square Park

I thought it might be a good idea to include another piece of my writing. It's also based on two very different characters, but this time I wanted to create a convincing sense of conflict between them. I've deliberately set the story in a tranquil setting to emphasise that conflict.

> *Bleached benches circled the tiny park occupied by office workers making the most of the early Spring day. Some ate their lunch, others read a book, and some lay back and simply raised their faces to the warmth of the mid-day sun. Nobody paid much attention to the two men seated near a statue in the centre of the park.*
>
> *The older of the two was a heavy man wearing an incongruous pork pie hat and a t-shirt at least one size too small for his protruding stomach. Stranger still, a dog-eared Bible lay open on the bench beside him. Now and again he'd point at it, or clutch it in his fist and wave it at his younger companion, who eventually leapt to his feet and gestured aggressively at him.*
>
> *"Billy, for God's sake, sit down!" pleaded the older man.*
>
> *Billy was not to be appeased and began to pace up and down in a quiet rage.*
>
> *For all his growing anger, Billy looked a little ridiculous in his torn, skinny jeans and corduroy trapper hat with its furry flaps that bounced in comic fashion the more he shook his head. Throughout, he never let his angry gaze drop from his older companion who simmered on the park bench.*

In the piece above, I wanted first to create a distinct setting – one that was peaceful, calm and restful – at a particular time of day and a particular time of year. Before the first paragraph's finished, though, I've already introduced my two main characters. At this early stage, there's nothing to mark them out in any way.

The second paragraph begins by providing some clear details about the physical appearance of the older of the two men. In addition, I've included a slightly unusual detail to help arouse my reader's curiosity – the "dog-eared Bible". The inclusion of this small detail helps to move the narrative forward when in the final sentence of this paragraph, the older man is seen to wave it at the younger man. This, in turn, leads to the dramatic action of the younger man leaping to his feet in anger. Now the reader is hooked and is going to stick around to find out what's going on between the two men.

Next, a tiny but significant piece of dialogue from the older man, the word "pleaded" suggesting a desire to resolve their differences. It's significant, too, because I've used it to casually provide the name of the younger man which allows me, in the next paragraph, to set up a contrast with the older man by describing details of "Billy's" appearance, movements and gestures.

By the end of this section, you know for sure that there's trouble brewing between these two very different men.

My challenge now is to turn up the heat in this argument between the two by using dialogue a little more and continuing to emphasise the difference between the two men. I also need to keep the narrative moving forward and maintain the interest of my readers.

> *Finally, Billy erupted.*
>
> *"I will not sit down!" he screamed.*
>
> *All around the quiet little park, eyes darted in Billy's direction as he flung his arms around. One or two office workers decided that lunch was now over and got up to leave.*
>
> *"How dare you wave that Bible at me. I will not listen to your lectures any more. You're a big old hypocrite, Tom!" Billy continued his rant.*
>
> *Tom perched himself on the edge of the bench shaking, his swollen, red face imploring Billy to sit down and talk things through quietly.*
>
> *"The way you've treated Dad is beyond cruel, Tom, and I won't be a part of it any longer," Billy roared.*
>
> *"I had no choice, Billy, believe me," Tom said, "he's lost the plot."*
>
> *"It's you that's lost the plot!" yelled Billy.*

And that's where I'm leaving it for now. I've made it clear that Billy and Tom, for all the physical differences between them, are actually brothers.

I've turned up the heat a little by choosing different verbs to describe how they speak to each other. Notice that Billy "*screamed*", "*roared*" and finally "*yelled*", whereas, defensive Tom merely "*said*" his words.

The use of quite heated dialogue is what creates the drama in this short scene. It also helps to inject pace into my story. But as ever, you need to be careful to keep a tight rein on your dialogue and not let it run away with you.

Hopefully I've left some questions unanswered, too, about the nature of their relationship as well as about their father's situation that seems to be at the heart of the dispute between them.

Finally, I've reminded the reader of the setting and the office workers on their lunch breaks who I'd referred to right at the start.

Why don't you try to continue writing the story of Billy and Tom?

Abingdon Square Park 43

Structure

In the GCSE English examination there will often be a question about '***structure***' in which you're expected to comment in detail on how a writer has put a piece of writing together in order to '*interest the reader*'.

It can be helpful to think of two sides of a coin here.

On one side, there's a piece of writing to read and analyse in terms of the way the writer has structured it. Here we need to think about how we're responding as readers.

On the other side of the coin is the business of writing itself and the choices a writer makes when it comes to putting the piece together, with more than one eye on creating interest for the reader.

For the purposes of this book, I'm going to focus on the second side of the coin. I want to go through a piece of my writing and explore the structural choices I made.

Have you ever completed a jigsaw? People have their own particular way of doing this but ultimately there's only one correct way to assemble a jigsaw for all the pieces fall into place.

Writing is different.

There are almost endless ways in which we can structure our writing.

Here are two paragraphs of my writing. In fact, it's the first and last paragraphs from about a page of that writing.

> **Read this opening paragraph first and jot down a note as follows:**
>
> *'At the beginning…"*
>
> **Write down a few things that you notice happening at the beginning of the story.**

> *I put a hat and scarf on and headed out of my apartment. Entering the lift, I pressed for the ground floor. The doors eased shut and with a gentle hush it descended the five floors to the ground. Outside, dusk had settled. A large man in a black, padded winter jacket went past leading a pack of sullen, emaciated dogs at a cruel pace along the wet pavement. Rain had soaked the streets and the dank, evening air let out a fetid sigh.*

....

....

....

....

....

Now read this final paragraph and jot down a note as follows:

'At the end …"

Write down a few things that you notice happening at the end of the story.

Back on the ground floor I found another homeless person arranging some cardboard and old newspapers into her bed for the night. "Excuse me," I said, "have you ever seen Kugan O'Connor? Number 12?" "Best for both of us," she shot back without looking at me, "if I don't answer that question."

Now put the notes you made on each paragraph side by side and see what you notice. Probably one of the following:

- A change
- A development
- A circling back to the beginning

So what have you already spotted about the way this piece of writing develops from start to finish?

Although I've written the paragraphs, here are some of my ideas. See if they're similar to yours.

At the beginning, the main character puts some warm clothes on and heads out of his apartment. He uses the lift first and once he gets to the ground floor, he notices it's now gone dark outside. He also notices an unpleasant man with a group of undernourished dogs that he's walking on the wet pavement.

At the end, the main character seems to have encountered a homeless person settling down for the night. There is a brief exchange between them in which the main character asks about someone called Kugan O'Connor. The homeless person makes a reply which seems to contain a warning about not enquiring too much about Kugan.

- The main character suddenly seems very inquisitive about a person called Kugan
- Some tension builds at the end as a result of the brief exchange with the homeless person
- A question is raised in the reader's mind about the character of Kugan – he seems to be a little dangerous or sinister perhaps
- The emaciated dogs and the homeless people seem to be part of some unknown pattern at this stage

Now take a look at the full piece of writing and continue with the same approach

- *At the beginning …*
- *And …*
- *But …*
- *By the end …*

When writing, try to think about why, and how, the writer has done certain things at particular parts of the story. If you do this, it'll help you to stay focused on the idea of structure rather than just wandering off to talk about language.

I put on a hat and scarf and headed out of my apartment. Entering the lift, I pressed for the ground floor. The doors eased shut and with a gentle hush it descended the five floors to the ground. Outside, dusk had settled. A large man in a black, padded winter jacket went past leading a pack of sullen, emaciated dogs at a cruel pace along the wet pavement. Rain had soaked the streets and the dank, evening air let out a fetid sigh.

As I arrived at Kugan's apartment block I was startled by a sudden movement from below. A homeless person, sensing my arrival and confusion at the array of buzzers in front of me, shifted to turn their hooded face away, but not before muttering darkly;

"Kugan? Number twelve."

I dropped some change beside the man, noticing that my hand was now shaking a little. I pressed for Kugan's apartment and a buzzer belched its permission. I walked inside the stainless steel lair. Not wanting to announce my arrival, I opted for the chill of the concrete stairwell instead. I arrived outside Kugan's front door.

I could hear what I imagined was the rhythmic sound of his fists furiously battering a small punch bag inside his hallway. I rang the bell and heard the punching cease. Silence. Then a dull burst of tough-talking rap music – Kugan's ring tone – followed by a loud cough as he cleared his throat to answer the call. He could just as easily have answered the door to me, still sweating from his exertions with the punch bag.

I froze, straining to hear what was being said just a few yards away on the other side of the door. I could hear his bare feet padding nimbly from room to room as he carried on the phone conversation. Time slowed down. It felt like I'd been there hours, when in fact it was only a matter of a few minutes. I could feel my heart thumping in my chest. Without warning, the conversation indoors ended and a door slammed shut. He was heading towards me. I turned and ran.

Back on the ground floor I found another homeless person arranging some cardboard and old newspapers into her bed for the night.

"Excuse me," I said, "have you ever seen Kugan O'Connor? Number 12?"

"Best for both of us," she shot back without looking at me, "if I don't answer that question."

Here's a commentary on some of the choices I made.

Let's start with the opening line:

> *I put on a hat and scarf and headed out of my apartment.*

A simple enough sentence. And that's a deliberate choice for starters. I want to create a sense of things being pretty normal as my main character gets dressed to go out. You'll also notice that I've opted for a first person narrative too – "I" and "my" are used in that first sentence. This can be important for helping to take my reader/s up close to the thoughts, feelings and actions of my main character.

Another simple sentence follows:

> *Entering the lift, I pressed for the ground floor.*

My first person narrator is quietly in charge of events here. Nothing startling but perhaps I'm thinking of setting up a contrast. Maybe later in the passage he's not in control quite as much as he'd like to be. A contrast is a really effective feature in your writing when it comes to structure; it allows your reader to notice any change you've introduced.

OK, here's the third sentence:

> *The doors eased shut and with a gentle hush it descended the five floors to the ground.*

As with the two previous sentences, there's nothing dramatic going on here which is exactly what I want to achieve at this stage in the narrative. I'm reinforcing the mood of calm and ordinariness with my choice of language to describe the lift's movements. In addition, I've incidentally provided the reader with a little more detail about my main character's circumstances – his home is on the fifth floor of an apartment block. Not too important you may think, but remember, I've got to make my readers interested in him. I've got to flesh out some details about his life. A detail about him living on the fifth floor revealed almost incidentally does just this.

Then a short sentence in mid-paragraph:

> *Outside, dusk had settled.*

As the writer, I've now removed my main character (and my readers) from the warmth and safety of his fifth floor apartment indoors.

He's now '*Outside*' and it's '*dusk*'. I've given the reader a moment to take stock and soak up the evening atmosphere. But I want to boost the pace of my narrative now and move things along quickly and introduce a slightly unnerving detail that doesn't seem to fit with the normal run of events so far. See what you think:

> *A large man in a black, padded winter jacket went past leading a pack of sullen, emaciated dogs at a cruel pace along the wet pavement.*

A '*large man*', '*sullen, emaciated dogs*', a '*cruel*' pace and a '*wet*' pavement.

This is a world away from the plain, almost bland sentences I've chosen to use so far. Now I want to give my reader a bit of a jolt. I want to keep them on their toes. My decision to suddenly include some threatening, unpleasant, descriptive content ought to put my readers on their guard. To round this first paragraph off, I've chosen to add another descriptive sentence to reinforce the emerging sense of danger:

> *Rain had soaked the streets and the dank, evening air let out a fetid sigh.*

I've engineered a rather tense and gloomy mood and in so doing, set the scene for the events that will unfold in the next few paragraphs. I'm hoping I've made my reader start to feel a bit uncomfortable.

Rather than going through the next few paragraphs in quite the same amount of detail, I want to look at each one more broadly to consider the structural choices and changes that I've made. Here's the second paragraph:

> *As I arrived at Kugan's apartment block I was startled by a sudden movement from below. A homeless person, sensing my arrival and confusion at the array of buzzers in front of me, shifted to turn their hooded face away, but not before muttering darkly, "Kugan? Number twelve." I dropped some change beside the man, noticing that my hand was now shaking a little. I pressed for Kugan's apartment and a buzzer belched its permission. I walked inside the stainless steel lair. Not wanting to announce my arrival, I opted for the chill of the concrete stairwell instead. I arrived outside Kugan's front door.*

I've continued with the first person narrator and introduced a different location – 'Kugan's apartment block'. I've continued to add to the sense of tension and threat by including various key details about the homeless person he encounters. I wanted to use some actual words from the homeless person to help add realism and credibility to the narrative. As for that narrative, I've chosen this moment to pile on several key details:

- my hand was now shaking a little
- I walked inside the stainless steel lair
- Not wanting to announce my arrival, I opted for the chill of the concrete stairwell

My intention was to really build a sense of fear and danger in the reader's mind.

Then I've added *a* dramatic cliffhanger at the end of the second paragraph for good measure:

> *'I arrive outside Kugan's front door.'*

What's going to happen next? Will our narrator be safe? Who's Kugan?

Let's take a look at the third paragraph to see how I've sustained my reader's interest in the situation my main character finds himself in:

> *I could hear what I imagined was the rhythmic sound of his fists furiously battering a small punch bag inside his hallway. I rang the bell and heard the punching cease. Silence. Then a dull burst of tough-talking rap music – Kugan's ring tone – followed by a loud cough as he cleared his throat to answer the call. He could just as easily have answered the door to me, still sweating from his exertions with the punch bag.*

From the start, I wanted to build suspense by shifting from the use of the visual sense (see paragraph one) to the sense of hearing. This paragraph is almost structured as a list of sounds the main character can hear;

- the rhythmic sound of his fists
- the ring of the bell
- silence
- a dull burst of tough talking rap music
- a loud cough

And, of course, all of these sounds contain within them the sense of threat and violence that was introduced in the previous paragraph. It seems a long time since my main character was in the safety of his own apartment. Remember the idea of contrast that I mentioned!

If you read back over this third paragraph, you'll notice that it's all about introducing the character of Kugan. Up until now, I've held back on anything about him. Now, through the details I've chosen to include at this stage, the reader ought to get the sense of a tough, physical and aggressive presence. But the reader will also notice that as part of the structure I've chosen, I'm actually holding back, almost teasing the reader, by failing to reveal anything else about Kugan. I don't allow the reader to see the other side of Kugan's front door! As a result of the way I've structured this, it means the reader has to actively use his or her imagination to visualise Kugan for themselves at this point.

The fourth paragraph continues to emphasise details gained through the sense of hearing;

- straining to hear
- I could hear his bare feet

Then I shake things up a little by placing the focus directly on my first person narrator and his thoughts and feelings. I want my reader to share in his fear and panic in the presence of Kugan. The fourth paragraph is rounded off with a short sentence and a dramatic moment as the narrator makes a hasty escape from danger;

'I turned and ran.'

Suddenly, I've brought the reader to my final paragraph. Now I need to make some careful choices about how to round things off. I decide to introduce another homeless person which gives a sense of events coming full circle. I also decide to use dialogue for the second time in the writing. Finally, I use more repetition by having a sense of menace and fear in the words of the homeless person replying to the main character.

Narrative Writing – Exemplar 1.

> **You have been asked to produce a piece of creative writing about nerves and being in danger; Write a story set in or close to a deserted shopping centre.**

Dan held his breath and counted to ten. He was determined not to panic. If he did, he knew his nerves would get the better of him – and that was too awful to contemplate. Slowly, he raised his head to peer over the wall at the sprawling concrete shopping centre below. Much of it was in shadow at this time of night.

He was sure he could see some surreptitious movement in the shadows near the steps leading up to his refuge on the fourth floor balcony. It couldn't possibly be Zoe down there. When they'd split up to get away from the gang, Zoe had run off towards the bus station, leaving Dan to fend for himself. He strained to listen for the sound of any footsteps.

All he could hear were some empty crisp packets and discarded plastic bottles swirling violently around the overflowing concrete bins in the corner. Suddenly, his eyes were sprayed with the gritty dust that was being whisked up by the chill breeze of this late September evening. For a moment or two he seemed to have lost his vision. Once again, he was teetering on the edge of a dangerous panic.

Taking stock, Dan removed one of his gloves and gently wiped at his eyes, careful not to aggravate matters any further. Relieved to have restored his vision, he nuzzled his chin deeper into the collar of his dark fleece away from the evening's chill – it was fast becoming his safety blanket. Time to peer over the balcony again, into the gloom.

On any given day, the shopping centre would be awash with people of all ages, going about their business. Large windows would gleam in the sunshine, their bright, colourful displays enticing shoppers to cross their thresholds. Meanwhile, upbeat music would blare, filling every corner of the wide walkways with sound. Dan knew every inch of the place – it was practically his second home.

But tonight was different.

Tonight it felt like a trap.

Or a cage from which there was no escape.

He sensed that feeling of nerves deep in his gut again, slowly starting to surface and rise into his throat. Dan distracted himself by looking for the shoe shop where he worked on Saturdays. Even in the dark he could could still make out the silhouette of the word 'SALE' on the enormous poster plastered in its window. He'd give anything to be serving awkward customers down there on a typical Saturday again, safe amongst his colleagues.

For someone who was doing a lot of observing from high above the shopping centre, it started to feel eerily like he was the one being watched. Then came the ominous thud of heavy footsteps on the stairs at the end of the landing. He began to think his fate was sealed.

"You alright, lad? What are you doing there?" came the voice.

He was too startled to answer. He froze.

"Dan, isn't it?" said the burly figure in a dark uniform, taking a closer look.

Suddenly, a warm rush of recognition raced through Dan's veins.

He could have cried.

It was Steve, one of the security team who patrolled the precinct day and night.

Commentary

- No dialogue at the start, thus placing a focus on the internal thoughts and emotions of the main character
- Gradual reveal; an explanation of the main character's circumstances in paragraph 2 – had been with his friend, Zoe – had escaped from a gang, plus a reference to his Saturday job in a shoe shop in paragraph 6

- Use of the senses to enhance the tension and give a sense of atmosphere – sound of the crisp packets and plastic bottles; touch – the feel of the grit in his eyes + the cold evening on his face; sight – the shadows, the silhouette, etc
- Use of contrast between the shopping centre at night time and during the day
- 2nd character – Zoe – has a subsidiary role – yet emphasises the nerves having run away
- Shift to short, simple sentences at the end of paragraph 5 to add to the sense of panic and urgency and the danger that Dan can now sense

Narrative Writing – Exemplar 2.

You are going to enter a creative writing competition. Your entry will be judged by a panel of people your own age. Write the opening part of a story about a place that has been damaged by a storm.

Ruth hadn't expected to find herself wearing a fish. Then again, there had been plenty of things that Ruth hadn't expected to happen this time last week. Had it really only been a week, she thought, since she'd begun boarding up her property ahead of the impending storm. A little flooding, a few trees down here and there, but Ruth had certainly not been ready for the sort of widespread chaos Storm Martha had brought. Including the fish that had fallen off the roof of her garage and onto the shoulder of her dirty overalls.

She gave the fish a long, quizzical look, and the fish returned the compliment with its dead eyes staring back at her; it probably hadn't been expecting to end its days this way. Martha had far exceeded all the usual storm warning expectations that this small, coastal community received as a matter of course as summer turned to autumn. In fact, as Martha first arrived, there was little to suggest she'd become a raging, shrieking harridan rather than a mildly annoyed old auntie.

It had been a long, terrifying night. The power had cut out around 6pm which been the prelude to the aggressive pounding of the winds as they whined and whistled across frail rooftops. Next came thunder and lightning, crackling violently over the land. Finally, the pitiless, pelting rain showered down with a noisy, wet thwack and gurgle.

Now there was just silence. Ruth's ears tried to take it in that the storm had actually passed. This was now the morning after and a strange, uncanny hush filled the narrow streets of St.Ervin. Removing the dead fish from her shoulder, she strode cautiously down the hill, careful to avoid the shards of broken glass and rusty nails sticking out of dislodged timbers. She felt like crying at the chaos opening up all around her.

To her left, just ahead, the old stone schoolhouse seemed intact. Ruth wondered how all the children who would normally be playing noisily in its yard, would be feeling this morning after witnessing the ferocity of the storm.

The schoolyard was bleak and empty this morning. And in the corner, near the gate, the sign with the Headteacher's name on it, lay crushed and battered by a hefty piece of fencing that had been uprooted and dumped there by the night's raging gale.

"Morning, Ruth,"

The warm, familiar greeting came from Jim Matthews, the local butcher. Strange that they should meet this morning of all mornings, Ruth thought, outside the school they'd both gone to as youngsters all those years ago. She wondered how Jim was coping with seeing their world turned upside down and so badly damaged.

"Morning, Jim. How are you and Mary doing?" Ruth replied.

"Not too bad thanks, Ruth. Mary's a little worried though, as she hasn't heard from her sister over in Tregullion yet," Jim said, "it took an even worse pounding than Saint Erv," calling their home by its affectionate, abbreviated form.

"I'm sure she'll be fine, Jim. I'll send Mary one of my apple pies round when things finally get back to normal," Ruth said in as cheery a voice as she could manage.

"You're an angel, Ruth," Jim replied," an absolute angel. Goodness knows, we're going to need all the help we can to get St.Erv' back on its feet."

"We'll manage, Jim, we'll manage," Ruth assured him.

She took his arm and the two old school friends who'd grown up together looked out across the tiny fishing village below. Yes, there'd been damage and destruction, but the quiet smiles on their faces said that St.Erv' would recover and live to see another day.

Commentary

- Bold, eye-catching opening line – "Ruth hadn't expected to find herself wearing a fish"
- Main character – Ruth – established very early in the narrative
- Clearly defined second character – Jim Matthews – a friendly face in the midst of the storm's aftermath
- Dialogue between Ruth and Jim helps to explore in more depth the impact of the storm
- Their dialogue also helps to begin to normalise things again after the harsh conditions of the previous night – it also helps to create a sense of a small, tight-knit community
- Contrast in paragraphs 3 and 4 between the noise and force of the storm and the calm and quiet of the next morning
- This was the opening to a story as the question had asked; it leaves off with scope for the writer to develop the story of the little fishing village's recovery after the storm
- There is also the option of the story being continued with a retrospective narrative

Narrative Writing – Exemplar 3.

Write the dramatic start to a mystery story

Now what? Kyle wondered.

Year 11 had already been on the receiving end of a savage roasting from Mr Marsh, their year tutor, in assembly this morning. Now here he was again with the same grim frown seared across his brow. Maths certainly wasn't Kyle's favourite subject but he resented the interruption to the familiar slog of simultaneous equations after lunch on Thursdays.

"... so just to be on the safe side, I've made the decision to close the school early this afternoon. I'll leave your teacher to dismiss you quietly in the next ten minutes," said Mr Marsh, before vanishing.

"Ok everyone, calm down. Pack your things away. As soon as you're all quiet, I'll let you go," said their long-suffering Maths teacher, Miss King.

Instead of making his way downstairs with his classmates when they'd been dismissed, Kyle headed up to the top floor. He'd brought an old games console in for Terri, the lab technician, to try to fix and he wanted to see how she was getting on with it. She was based in a small prep room at the back of the physics lab; he was sure she wouldn't mind him dropping by. If he was lucky, she might even make him a cup of tea!

The top floor was always a little dark but now it was deserted and strangely quiet too. The only sound was the squeaky plod of Kyle's shoes on the worn, polished floor. Kyle increased his pace and counted the classroom doors as he made his way down the long, forbidding corridor. A light fitting flickered erratically in the distance. Josh let out an involuntary shudder.

What was the matter with him, he thought.

Terri could hear the steps making their way towards where she was being held captive and did her best to make some noise. The thick, sticky duct tape over her mouth made this almost impossible.

Maybe if she tried to bang her bound feet together on the floor that might work, she thought.

Then before she could move, she spotted a little light soaking into the room as the door to her prep room opened gingerly. Her heart pounded hard and heavy in her chest and she shut her eyes tight to block out the inevitable.

"Terri!" Kyle gasped.

Terri dared to open her eyes and was rewarded with the sight of an astonished Kyle.

"What on earth's going on? Are you ok?" Kyle stuttered.

Suddenly more aware of the reality of Terri's predicament, Kyle moved forward and gently began to remove the tape from her mouth. Terri spat out a noisy sigh of relief.

"Kyle, quick, cut me loose, they could be back anytime."

Fumbling frantically with the large pair of scissors on the bench behind her, Kyle set about freeing Terri with as much haste as he could. He noticed his hands were shaking and his mouth felt much too dry; he'd have given anything for a can of Coke right now, he thought.

"… so just to be on the safe side, I've made the decision to close the school early this afternoon…"

Mr Marsh's words suddenly popped into his mind. What had the Head meant by 'just to be on the safe side'? Safe from what, Kyle wanted to know. Before he had time to think, Terri had taken him by the hand and led him into the adjacent physics lab.

The lab was in almost total darkness.

Except for a small red light flashing on a video camera mounted on a tripod at the front of the room.

Commentary

- Strong, bold start launches the reader straight into the narrative
- Quickly establishes the context and setting for the story
- Element of mystery introduced early with the slightly cryptic speech from Mr Marsh, the year tutor
- Introduction of Terri, the lab technician, as an effective second character
- Good range of punctuation throughout
- Shift from classroom to description of top floor adds to sense of mystery and suspense and propels the narrative forward
- Dramatic central moment in the narrative as Kyle discovers Terri, gagged and bound in the laboratory prep room
- Tense, short, rapid dialogue between Kyle and Terri adds to the sense of urgency and helps to deepen the mystery that is being prepared in the narrative
- Narrative almost comes full circle as Kyle recalls the cryptic words from Mr Marsh before the class were dismissed – this piece of narrative writing has an effective structure and introduces some key changes and developments at appropriate moments
- Cliffhanger at the end establishes something of the mystery and leaves plenty for the reader to speculate about

http://www.secretsofenglish.co.uk

Here's the start of a piece of *Narrative Writing* about a lunch time at school that ends in disaster.

Oliver sat rubbing his wet hair with a damp towel and a smirk on his face. All around the steamy changing room, his classmates were a good five minutes ahead of him. Most were now back in their uniforms, huddled together, chatting animatedly amongst themselves, laughing loudly and easily.

Much of their banter and chat was focused on the imminent school prom. Oliver listened with interest. It was going to be quite a night.

"Come on, Ol', hurry up, mate."

Like a puppet brought to life, Oliver suddenly jerked himself upright on the hard wooden bench. Trying hard to re-focus, he responded to his friend Charlie in a strangely hard, and peremptory voice;

"Be right with you."

Charlie maintained his cheery demeanour and shouted back;

"I should hope so too. We're going to be at the back of the lunch queue at this rate. Come on, mate, I'm starving!"

Now try to finish this opening part of a story.

Section 2

Descriptive Writing

First steps with descriptive writing

Let's take a look at the sort of question you could be asked in the exam.

I'll start with a reminder that there will often be a photograph used as the basis for the writing, such as the one below.

It's not the most exciting photo, right? And the question's tucked underneath it.

Write a description suggested by this picture.

So where do we start?

Your best bet is to jot down what you can see – in this case: clouds, boats, the shore, and a tide that's gone out.

At this stage, just keep it nice and simple.

How about this for a first attempt?

> *It was a cloudy day and the boats were sitting on the shore waiting for the tide to turn.*

On the plus side, I've used the image to good effect and what I've written describes what's in the photograph. It's not going to light any fires though, is it? It's bland and a little dull.

How can I improve on my first attempt?

Easy – just include some fairly basic adjectives to describe some of the things I've already noticed.

Here's my second attempt …

> ***Small** boats sat under **heavy** cloud on the **wide** shore waiting for a **strong** tide to return.*

That's better, right?

Now I want to think about the movement of the things that I'm noticing and have a go at using some more interesting adjectives and adverbs.

See what you think:

> ***Small, blue** fishing boats sat **awkwardly**, tilted under **drifting** banks of cloud on the **wide, damp** shore waiting for the **strong** surge of an incoming tide.*

Even better, yes?

I'm feeling confident enough to write my second line now and this time I'm going to include some *alliteration*, where words begin with the same letter or sound.

> *Only the **tired trickle** of an earlier tide remained to **tempt** hungry **sea-birds** to **search and scavenge** on the wet **sand**.*

You'll notice that I've added a little detail about some 'hungry sea-birds' – I couldn't actually see any on the photo, but remember, the question asked you to 'Write a description suggested by the picture.' And that's exactly what I've done by including the detail about the sea-birds.

Here are the first two sentences together:

> *Small, blue fishing boats sat awkwardly, tilted under drifting banks of cloud on the wide, damp shore waiting for the strong surge of an incoming tide. Only the tired trickle of an earlier tide remained to tempt hungry sea-birds to search and scavenge on the wet sand.*

Not bad, though I say it myself.

Try writing your own paragraph of descriptive writing based on the photograph on the earlier page.

Some ideas for using the senses in descriptive writing

Growing up surrounded by the media in its various forms, we're all used to letting the visual images on our screens do the talking. It's great to be able to see in detail and high definition the reality of life in a small village in India, the perils of plastics in far flung oceans, or dramatic events closer to home. The visual media can transport us anywhere.

The same is true of good descriptive writing and it has the added advantage of allowing the reader's imagination to come into play. If this is to work, our goal as writers should be to write with conviction and clarity.

And that's where the senses play their part.

Quick reminder – there are 5 of them – ***sight***, ***sound***, ***smell***, ***taste*** and ***touch or feel***.

Try to get into the habit of noticing which of the senses you're detecting. You can do this wherever you are. Here are a few instances I've logged recently.

Standing at the bus stop in the rain

- sight of the green trees overhanging the bus shelter
- ***sound of the traffic going past***
- feel of the rain dripping through the trees

Walking along the waterfront

- sight of a ferry ploughing its way up the river
- sound of seagulls soaring in the sky
- ***feel of the breeze on my face***
- smell of the salt sea air

In the Office

- ***smell of fresh coffee brewing***
- sound of background music playing
- sight of rows of desks

You'll see that I've not noticed the sense of **taste** in any of the examples above.

I've also highlighted in bold font, in each example, the one sense that was more noticeable than the others. If I was attempting to write a descriptive paragraph about any one of the scenarios above, I'd almost certainly focus on the dominant, most noticeable sense.

For example, if I was writing about '***Standing at the bus stop in the rain***', this is what I might write:

> *A young woman squeezed under the roof of the bus shelter, adjusted the collar of her mac, and shook the rain off her umbrella. This morning's downpour had been a heavy one and seemed to exaggerate the noise of the passing traffic on the busy road. Cars whistled past and lorries roared along, the thud of their axles reverberating as they hit bumps and potholes. A rowdy rush of tyres slurped noisily and spat the spray from the wet surface, soaking any unsuspecting passers-by.*

Although I've referred to the rain and a fellow occupant of the bus-shelter at the start, by the second sentence, I've shifted my attention to the noise of the traffic and maintained this focus through to the end of the paragraph. I wanted my readers to be left in no doubt about the level of the traffic's noise. By emphasising this particular sense, I hope I've created a credible scene.

Specifically, here's what I included in the writing above:

- A simple, factual statement about how the weather ***exaggerated the noise of the passing traffic*** – I've drawn the reader's attention to the noise
- The choice of two interesting verbs to describe the noise of the cars and the lorries – ***whistled*** and ***roared*** – simultaneously creating a contrast between the noise of the two different types of vehicles – both verbs stress the din of the traffic

- I've gone for something a little more dramatic next with the use of the word ***thud*** to describe their axles hitting the potholes and bumps – a much deeper, resonating sound that almost hints at an underlying violence and danger in the scene as the traffic barrels along
- Next some alliteration – first the ***rowdy rush*** followed by ***slurped***, ***spat*** and ***spray*** to reinforce the drivers' selfish lack of consideration for pedestrians

As I've mentioned before, you could be given a photograph to use as the basis for your descriptive writing. Now might be a good time to see how you can make the connection between a photograph and the senses.

Take a look at the one above – it's a photograph of a skateboard park in **Liverpool's Baltic Quarter**.

Just like before, start logging the senses we might expect to experience here.

- *sight of colourful graffiti*
- *sight of stains on the concrete surfaces*
- sound of traffic
- sound of skateboarders

You'll notice that I've included the sound of two things that aren't really present in the photo – passing traffic and skateboarders. That's fine as the question will usually ask you to produce a piece of descriptive writing **suggested by the photograph**.

I think it's reasonable to include these sounds, don't you?

On the other hand, I'm struggling a bit to come up with anything connected with the senses of touch, taste or smell at this point so I'm going to focus on the other two senses.

For me, the dominant sense here is the sight of the colourful graffiti contrasting with the sight of stains on the concrete.

Now I need to think of simple ways of describing the **colours of the graffiti**.

Here are three simple adjectives for starters:

- bright
- vivid
- bold

Nothing wrong with any of them but I'm going to try to be a bit more ambitious now:

- dazzling
- radiant
- dramatic

Next I need to do the same for the sight of the ***stains on the concrete***:

- wet
- damp
- dirty

And

- saturated
- soaked
- grimy

Finally, I'm going to try to produce a paragraph of descriptive writing drawing on some of what I've jotted down above:

> *The sharp silhouettes of a group of teenage skateboarders flashed swiftly across the concrete of the urban skatepark, stained and saturated with a greasy film of filth. All around, dazzling graffiti wrapped the walls of dirty, derelict buildings that towered above them. Bold, vivid blocks of colour radiated out across the skatepark, a dramatic accompaniment to the energy and flair of the skateboarders rattling noisily by on the damp, uneven surface.*

Take a closer look at the paragraph of descriptive writing above and you'll see that I've used material from each of the lists. Nothing's gone to waste.

Just as importantly, I've not allowed myself to be boxed in by the lists. I've introduced new ideas and ways of describing the stains on the concrete, the colours of the graffiti, and the scene as a whole. I think it works quite well.

http://www.secretsofenglish.co.uk

Now it's your turn

Take a look at the photograph below and follow the steps I've outlined above:

- Study the photograph
- Log the senses that you notice playing a part in the image
- Try to decide what the dominant sense is
- Now try to decide on words that help to describe that sense

Based on the ideas that you've jotted down, have a go at a paragraph of descriptive writing based on the photo above.

Now it's your turn

Descriptive writing
– first responses to a photograph

This one shows the Vale of Clwyd in North Wales on an afternoon in late August a few years ago. It had been a warm, summer's day but the weather was clearly about to change. As my car climbed higher up the range of hills above, I pulled in and took this photo. I wish I'd been able to take a photo 30 minutes earlier, too, as a way of showing the dramatic contrast that had appeared.

Just remember, it's photos exactly like this one that could appear as the basis of a piece of narrative or descriptive writing on your GCSE English exam paper.

Descriptive writing – first responses to a photograph   77

You may well get a choice of questions like those below.

1. Write a description suggested by this picture

or

2. Write the opening part of a story about a place that is severely affected by the weather.

You'll have around 45 minutes or so to answer a question like this and there will be a lot of marks riding on it too.

And those 45 minutes will have included planning time, too, which the examiner likes to see evidence of.

So you need to get moving and approach the question as efficiently as possible.

One way to do this is to break the image down into its various parts.

As you can see, this image breaks down into three quite distinct sections.

You can practice on any images that you might find to see how they break down into different sections.

In the meantime, let's take another look at the image we've been working on already by adding some of the things we can see in each of its three sections.

On the one hand, I'm just noticing things – clouds, sunlight, or the valley – but I'm also including just a little detail too, to describe the things that I've noticed.

Equipped with the above information and detail, I've got the makings of some really good material for a piece of descriptive writing. The question was quite an open one – **Write a description suggested by this picture** – the challenge now is to plan and arrange my ideas so that I can do this.

Descriptive writing
– shifting the perspective

Each of these three photographs were taken at the same spot on a crisp Autumn morning in the Dingle area of Liverpool. At first glance, there's not a lot to see.

Photo 1

So let's start by scrutinising each of the three photographs, logging what we notice.

Start by stating the obvious, I'd suggest. There's a road, some trees and a few cars parked up. Now let's push the boat out a little and be more specific. That road that we noticed, for example. It's actually quite a steep hill. Those trees, which are on both sides of the road – some of them, are a really bright, vivid green, but look more closely and we can see that the leaves are starting to turn.

This is early Autumn and some rich golden colours are breaking through. Look more closely still, and there's another clue that Autumn's on its way – the leaves are starting to appear on the ground and gather in the gutter at the kerbside. Look even more closely at the road and we can see some heavy shadows stretching out intermittently across the quiet road.

Photo 2

This is taken from the same spot across the road. But all of sudden, a whole new set of things appear. The road's still there and the pavements are cluttered with tall lampposts and street signs.

The bright green leaves of the trees are still there on the right, but the top of the image is framed by the dark silhouette of a branch full of leaves giving a different feel to the place – in my view, making it seem a little colder, a little chillier in spite of the Autumn sunshine. But suddenly we can see a river at the bottom of the road, with a few small boats floating on its calm surface. In the distance is the shore opposite and some hills emerging even further away.

Photo 3

Not a lot to see here.

Except there's something quite important to notice. It's the detail – the close up. Suddenly we're looking at the dark, heavy boughs of one of the trees in blurred silhouette and the shimmering leaves and light surrounding them.

From these 3 photographs taken at random from the same spot we're able to pull together quite a large haul of details.

What's also helped enormously is using the simple technique of shifting the perspective so that we get a richer picture which allows us as writers to move on to form some impressions.

> **Here are 3 more photographs for you to practise with using the approach I've just explained above. Remember, it's simply a way for you to think visually and to generate ideas.**

Photo 1

What can you see in Photo 1 – jot your ideas down here.

....

....

....

Photo 2

All three photographs are taken at Saltburn-by-the-sea in the North East of England. Each one is taken from a different perspective. What can you see in the second photograph that you couldn't in the first one? Jot your ideas down below.

Photo 3

Now jot down what you can see in Photo 3.

Interrogating the image

Photo 1.

Take a look at this image.

I want to focus on this as a starting point for a few different approaches to your narrative/descriptive writing.

1. Creating mood and atmosphere
2. Finding clues for a narrative
3. Visualisation and imagination

Keep an open mind and try to be as responsive to the image as you can.

Think creatively.

1. Creating mood and atmosphere – Photo 2.

Sometimes it can help to think of opposites when it comes to mood and atmosphere. So below is a very different image.

These two columns might help to explain what I mean.

Try to go with your gut-feeling … your instinct … when it comes to the mood or atmosphere.

Photo 1	Photo 2
Sinister	Peaceful
Threatening	Tranquil
Intimidating	Calm
Gloomy	Serene

Strangely enough, both images show places that are really still with nobody in sight. And there's barely any movement, hardly a breath of air to be seen.

It can be just as helpful to jot down a couple of things you can't see too.

Once you've sorted out what you think the mood and atmosphere is, let's say calm and tranquil, your job is to convince the reader of this in your writing.

There are a few good ways you can do this.

First, it helps to use some detail that draws on the senses.

In Photo 2, we might write about how gently the reeds at the side of the lake move. Maybe even use some imagery, perhaps a metaphor to capture this.

Now lets build the sensory descriptive detail up a little by referring to the sense of sound. What sort of noises might we hear if we were standing on that spot?

> *The quiet lapping of the water rippling at the the edge of the lake.*

Or maybe the sound of …

> *A solitary curlew wading among the reeds and its haunting song a long drawn-out mournful bubbling.*

Suddenly we're building a credible and convincing mood and atmosphere for our reader. With luck, we've started to take them to the place we're writing about.

Now let's try the same approach on **Photo 1**.

I'm going to focus on the neon '*Motel*' sign for starters. I'm also going to need to use my imagination a little and tease out some detail by interrogating the image.

http://www.secretsofenglish.co.uk

> Q: What sort of area is this?
>
> Q: What sort of motel would be in an area like this?
>
> Q: How well maintained would the neon sign be?
>
> Q: What noise would a faulty neon sign make?
>
> Q: How can I suggest mood and atmosphere by focusing on this?

Here are my answers – not necessarily the right ones, of course.

It looks like a backstreet, perhaps a rather run down or slightly seedy area.

The motel would be a cheap and simple one. Certainly no luxuries here. It might even be a little run down too.

Assuming I'm on the right lines so far, then I doubt if anyone would be too bothered whether the neon sign should be maintained or not.

As for the sort of noise a faulty neon sign would make, it would be an erratic, or intermittent fizzing sound. Not a sound that would attract you to the motel. In fact, apart from the sound, there's a good chance the harsh neon light of the sign would be flickering too.

Aside from that, I'm probably going to add in some descriptive detail about the sound of some light traffic in the distance, perhaps even a siren. This is a city at night, I'd suggest, from what I can see in the photograph.

http://www.secretsofenglish.co.uk

Collating your responses to photographs

Earlier in the book we looked at how you can break down an image into its various parts as a way of planning and preparing to write a ***descriptive*** piece.

Here are two more images for you to practise on. Just follow these simple instructions:

- Think about how you're looking at the image – what are you noticing first?
- Now jot down as many things that you notice in the image, no matter how obvious or insignificant they may seem
- Finally, try to organise these details into the most sensible order you can, from the ones that stand out most, to the less obvious

Image 1

Image 2

Descriptive Writing – Exemplar 1.

> **Write a description of a place that means a lot to you.**

Winters can seem endless with their short days and rationed daylight. It's a time when life seems to be lived in chilly monochrome among the wet streets of the city, choked with fumes. Trees, naked and exposed to the elements, offer neither shelter nor sustenance. We crave the light, warmth and colour of long, summer days lived by the water.

The Aber Foreshore, just across the water from the ancient and imposing castle walls of Caernarfon, can easily wash away these dark memories of winter, as the healing light from its wide, blue skies pours out across fields, sands and rippling tides. Wet seaweed on the shore dries out, shrivels and cracks in its warmth.

A gentle sort of ease spreads all around.

Seabirds wheel and race on the the balmy thermals overhead while slender cloud trails scratch and carve their marks on the arching skies above. I liked to catch the warmth of the breeze on my face, gazing out at the usual horizon, eager for it to heal the winter's wounds. In the distance, a chugging pleasure boat dips and bounces through the waves of the Menai Straits, as they crash, foamy white against its bows.

The Straits glisten in the sun and its small tributaries glint as they trickle and run into the damp sand. I've spent many happy hours with a tiny net here, scooping up small fish, crabs and sea anemones from the dark, shallow rock pools that littered the shore when the tide ebbed. Each expedition seemed to bring a fresh surprise – sometimes a starfish prised from a narrow crevice, sometimes a handful of green seaweed was tipped dripping into my bucket.

Then the awkward stumble over the uneven carpet of rocks, pebbles and bleached driftwood, heading back up the gentle incline of the beach with the salty aroma of the sea in my nostrils. Something in the water of the Straits gave it a distinctive, briny tang unique to this incredible part of the coast; I happily gulped in each breath of the sea air.

Back on the narrow, grey lane that hugged the shore, with the sweet, musky smell of the sand on my hands, I'd take a pause and stare wide-eyed at the sharp, bright colours of the beach and water in front of me. In the distance, an island. It was the low tree line of Anglesey's shore calling out mysteriously from over the water. Its proximity across the treacherous Straits – so near, yet so far – only added to the wonder of the Aber Foreshore.

Meanwhile, behind me, ancient stone walls, sturdy and strong, looked out defiantly at the water. And behind the walls, dark green hedgerows, stubbornly guarding the sheep, cattle and crops of the farmers' fields. Best of all were the fields of freshly cut hay with their sweet, powdery smell wafting on the breeze. Now and again, the quiet of the day would be broken by a farmer's tractor rattling past, spitting out the oily smell of its diesel engine. Sometimes, if I was lucky and the farmer caught my eye, I'd be given a ride on the makeshift seat at the back of the tractor as it made its way to the farmhouse.

Once there, Mrs Owen, the farmer's wife, would pour some fresh, cold milk taken from their own herd earlier that day. Thick slices of warm toast made from her home made bread rounded off the mid-afternoon treat. I'd sit fascinated as she and her husband slipped effortlessly from speaking English to Welsh and back again to English, smiling at me all the while. Somehow, this seemed to capture the magic of the place which has remained important to me all my life.

Commentary

- The writing uses all of the senses; touch, taste, smell, hearing and vision.
- The writing zooms in and zooms out; sometimes to describe a wide scene or panorama – for example, the "wide, blue skies". At other times, the writing zooms in on much smaller details – for example, the description of the "Wet seaweed" on the shore
- The writing has attempted to use interesting adjectives such as "the balmy thermals", the "awkward stumble", or the "sturdy and strong" stone walls
- The writing has attempted to use powerful verbs that make an impact on the reader such as – "shrivels and cracks"

- Shifting between different areas in this place maintains the reader's interest
- The writing also includes some internal thoughts to add credibility and to. enhance the quality of the description.

These are the notes I made before I wrote the piece above. You will notice that I've not included everything and sometimes I've written about things that weren't in my notes. Also, I have not necessarily followed the order in which I've jotted down my ideas. You may not have time to produce as much as this in your planning in the exam but it might give you an idea how could approach this type of writing.

Write a description of a place that means a lot to you.

- Wide skies
- Scale of the natural surroundings dwarfs human life and activity
- Dramatic cloud formations and trails scratched on the sky
- Silver glint and shine of tracks of water on the shore
- Salt smell of the Straits
- Colours
- Backdrop of the mountains
- Quiet lane alongside the shore – grey winding ribbon
- Breeze
- Distant shore of Anglesey
- Occasional pleasure boat
- Occasional rescue helicopter's reassuring presence
- Wet and dry seaweed
- Stranded pieces of twisted and warped driftwood
- Purple plant fronds and tough grasses
- Sharp, bright colours blend and meander out into the Straits
- Small dark silhouettes of seabirds
- Fierce, stubborn, ancient hedgerows

- Memories
- Tranquil
- Be alone with my thoughts
- Restorative
- Inspiration
- Creative
- Immersive – lost in the dramatic simplicity of the place

It can pay to practise jotting your ideas down in response to a question.

Descriptive Writing – Exemplar 2.

Write a description suggested by this picture

The sudden snowfall had been heavy and hard, taking the city by surprise. Just yesterday, clear spring sunshine had warmed the ground and the first sign of green leaves had started to appear on the trees in the park. Walking to work, locals had discarded their thick coats and scarves, and raised their eager faces to the bright blue skies.

Yesterday's vivid colours had now been drained and replaced by the shocking, intense white of the snow, throwing itself at a city caught off guard. Heads were buried in hoods again and bodies were wrapped to repel the penetrating, frozen chill of winter's last vicious surge. Naked faces froze, exposed to the frosty air once more.

Some sat huddled, thawing in warm cafes, breathing in rich fumes of roasting coffee and freshly baked donuts, glancing through windows fogged and dripping damp with condensation. Now and then, the pedestrian crossing signal on the busy street outside would flash from red to green and a diagonal mob of cold commuters would push across to the other side, moving as one.

Stationary traffic pulsed listlessly at the crossing as engines idled and their fumes leaked into the air. Further down the street came the muffled sound of car horns, while heavy buses, laden with passengers, lumbered and shunted along through the wet, grey snow, airbrakes hissing and wheezing as they went. Sensing their approach, pedestrians were drawn, magnet-like, to the far side of the wide pavements, avoiding the drowning splash and burst of water from buses' tyres as they bounced past.

In spite of their best efforts, though, people's shoes became damp and their shoulders shawled with a frosted dandruff. One or two shuffled across to a lone news vendor who sat insulated and layered and shrugged off the morning's biting chill, his papers weighted and secured on the icy metal stall. Cold coins were dropped in his hand and papers quickly stashed in bags and briefcases.

The headlines on the papers yelled the shocking news about the unexpected winter storm – plunging temperatures and pounding snow – with no respite on the horizon for this urban fridge. The city had beaten a retreat; shops rolled up their canvas awnings; smart hotel doormen stood at their posts and stamped their freezing feet; people walked their padded, quilted dogs with grim determination.

At the kerbside, a pair of sturdy bikes stood locked, propped and tethered to a lampost, their baskets empty save for the small mounds of snow that had deposited itself there. The spokes lay still in their large wheels. Whoever owned these bikes had no use for them while the snow lay all around. Only when the storm passed would these silhouetted forms resume their duties.

Commentary

- Notice that the photograph has acted as a springboard – the bicycles aren't actually mentioned until the final paragraph, although there's plenty of reference to the heavy snow right from the start
- A helpful contrast regarding the very different weather conditions over previous days adds to the idea of the snowstorm having caught everybody by surprise and of how cold it has now become
- The contrast works not only in terms of the very different temperatures but also in terms of the very different colours before and after the snowstorm
- Sense of the city being vulnerable in the face of the snowstorm has been created – "taking the city by surprise" and "a city caught off guard"
- Some alliteration at the end of the second paragraph to reinforce the idea of the biting cold – "Naked faces froze, exposed to the frosty air"
- The writing has focused on a number of senses – touch in paragraph 1, sight in paragraph 2, and smell in paragraph 3
- Interesting observational details are used in the description – "a diagonal mob of cold commuters would push across to the other side, moving as one" in paragraph 3 for example, or "people walked their padded, quilted dogs with grim determination" in paragraph 6
- Clear links between individual paragraphs through the use of topic sentences, such as between paragraphs 5 and 6 – "Cold coins were dropped in his hand and papers quickly stashed in bags and briefcases" is mentioned at the end of paragraph 5 with regard to the news vendor and then at the start of paragraph 6 we have – "The headlines on the papers yelled the shocking news about the unexpected winter storm" – and the focus shifts from the news vendor to the newspaper headlines

Descriptive Writing – Exemplar 3.

Write a description suggested by this picture

Adjusting a soft, worn cushion behind me, I leaned back and took in my surroundings at this latest berth. I wasn't used to seeing quite so many people at large on a towpath. Then again, my battered, old canal boat didn't usually venture into cities or towns. Certainly there were plenty of trees and bushes around here, but look a little closer at the foliage and the warehouses, offices and apartment blocks soon came into view amongst them.

High above me, I could hear light, summer tunes coming from a radio, interrupted now and then by laughter and chat from the occupants of the smart balconies. Here and there, tanned limbs poked through the railings, soaking up the warmth of the midday sun, while an array of privileged faces, masked by glossy, black sunglasses lazily scanned their high-rise vistas.

Down here, shaded from the sun, the canal boat sat gently on the lapping water, its roof cluttered with my assorted possessions in crumpled plastic bags and old cardboard boxes. Propped against this disorderly pile lay my rusting bike, carefully roped and secured. Perhaps later, if I could shake off the lethargic ease of a summer's day, I would ride to the nearest supermarket to scour for reduced items.

I watched patiently for clues among the passing pedestrians. Some were carrying heavy bags bulging with shopping, perhaps from that supermarket. Which direction were they coming from, I wondered? For now, they seemed more intent on making the most of their leisure time, ambling along, than on the loads they were carrying.

Now and again, I'd catch one of them casting a curious eye in the direction of my boat; what were they thinking as they saw the owner of this oddly worn and domesticated craft draped over the stern, with a mug of steaming tea in his hand? Would they be able to smell the warm, burnt toast coming from my boat's galley? Nothing tasted better in my opinion!

For me, it was occasional ducks that caught my attention, gliding in their family formations and weaving among the mooring ropes from the assembled boats tethered to the towpath. These passing ducks left thin, dark trails that sliced through the dimpled surface of the water, causing the gentlest of ripples, moving with enviable ease and with a clear sense of direction.

Turning my gaze behind me, I watched as a film of oily liquid seeped surreptitiously into the canal from my boat and felt a sudden rush of shame. We didn't belong here, that much was clear.

Commentary

- This descriptive piece sits within a narrative framework which has helped to provide a shape and a structure for the writing
- The structure of the writing is also helped by the developing contrast between the conditions of the narrator's life and what he sees in the environment in which he finds himself
- Effective and accurate use of paragraphing to support the structure of this descriptive piece of writing
- The writing has used the internal thoughts and observations of the narrator to generate the descriptive detail of the piece
- There is a clear movement between various aspects of the scene in the photograph – the boat, the canal, the trees and the buildings beyond the towpath
- The writing has made good use of a range of senses – touch (the feel of the cushion in the opening line), sight (the initial observations made all the way through to noticing the oily liquid coming from his boat), sound (the noise of summer music coming from a distant radio), smell (the warm, burnt toast)
- A range of punctuation has been used accurately throughout the piece

http://www.secretsofenglish.co.uk

I hope you've enjoyed the book and found it useful.

Why not follow me on
Instagram : **secretsofenglish**
Twitter : **@secretsofengli1**

Or visit the website:
http://www.secretsofenglish.co.uk

NOTES

NOTES

Printed in Great Britain
by Amazon